TEXTS BY LAURE VERCHÈRE
PHOTOGRAPHS BY LAZIZ HAMANI

ANTIQUAIRES

PARIS FLEA MARKETS

ASSOULINE

This book is for my children, who have enlightened me
and taught me to see the world through inspired eyes.
They have lifted away the gray hue from my world so that
I may finally see the color of the world that will be theirs.
For my three sons, Yannis, Mathis, and Nohna: I love you.
—LAZIZ HAMANI

© 2010 Assouline Publishing
601 West 26th Street, 18th Floor
New York, NY 10001, USA
www.assouline.com

© Photographs by Laziz Hamani/Éditions Assouline, Paris.
Translated from the French by Denise Raab Jacobs

ISBN : 978 2 7594 0460 5

Graphic design: Nelly Riedel

Color separation: Planète Couleurs (France)
Printed by in Italy by Grafiche Milani

FOREWORD

I will never forget the first time I saw the flea markets of Paris.

It was 1999; I was in my early thirties and had decided to reimagine my life. So I did what all romantics dream of doing—I moved to Paris. During my first week there, a good friend, who had spent many of her formative years in Paris, flew in to show me the ropes. With an empty Left Bank apartment and a full wallet (I had just sold my San Francisco home before the dot-com bubble burst), we went shopping. Our first stop was Clignancourt, at the foot of Saint-Ouen, the famous Paris flea market.

Within minutes of arriving, I knew this was the beating heart of design and collecting. On the spot, I decided I would find a way to turn this into a career. Like all bleary-eyed, jet-lagged Americans arriving at the flea market for the first time, I felt like Columbus discovering the New World—I was going to bring the flea markets of Paris to the world via the Internet.

I hired a photographer and a computer programmer—both of whom are French and, ten years later, still work for us—and I made a new friend who could translate. At the time, I barely spoke a word of French, which, as it turns out, was not all that necessary. The dealers at the flea markets know how to make a sale in any language.

Our fate was sealed with the tragedy of the September 11, 2001, terrorist attacks, which essentially shut down international travel; the only way for Americans to visit Paris was virtually. No sales were made in the first week after the attacks. Then, suddenly, the sales began rolling in. The months that followed were, to this day, our busiest. It was clear that Americans were addicted to French design—and if they couldn't go to the flea markets in person, they would buy it online.

I made it my mission to unearth the most unique treasures for them. I would rise before dawn every Friday to peruse the flea markets, cataloguing our favorite dealers' latest finds so people around the world could, every week, shop the famed flea markets on 1stdibs.

Still, after ten years of weekly visits to Clignancourt and having listed more than 75,000 items, I realize there is nothing like being there. Finding that one special item stacked behind something, obscured so that nobody else has spotted it, or seeing the theater of display of which only the French are capable, can only be appreciated in person. But if you can't make a trip to the Paris flea markets, you can still see for yourself by turning the pages of this exceptional book. While it may not be the same as being there, it's the next best thing.

MICHAEL BRUNO
Founder and CEO, 1stdibs

TABLE OF CONTENTS

CHAPTER 1 | The History of *les puces*

P. 12   From the Court of Miracles
         to an official beginning
P. 12   The antiques business takes off
P. 16   From the Vernaison Market to the Biron Market:
         dealers face many difficulties
P. 16   Surrealism finds an ally;
         conformism is abandoned
P. 21   An endless source of inspiration
P. 22   Madeleine Castaing, the "Queen of *les puces*"
P. 22   A time of frivolity for Bérard and Dior
P. 24   The bric-a-brac style of Louise de Vilmorin
P. 24   Luxury, according to Coco Chanel
P. 24   The exuberant Rudolf Nureyev
P. 27   Dealers find their calling
P. 27   The spirit of *les puces*

CHAPTER 2 | The Classic

P. 33   Marianne and Albert Rodriguez
P. 33   Léon Benaïm
P. 34   Jane and Nicholas Moufflet
P. 34   Françoise-Anne and François Bachelier
P. 34   Laurence and Henri Veyrier
P. 41   Janine Giovannoni
P. 41   Patrick Morcos
P. 41   La Maison James
P. 44   Huguette Portefaix

CHAPTER 3 | The Modern

P. 91   Marie and Cyril Grizot
P. 95   Guilhem Faget
P. 95   Pascal Cuisinier
P. 95   Raphaël Druet
P. 96   Gilles Oudin
P. 96   Yann Guérin
P. 96   Nicolas Giovannoni
P. 98   La Petite Maison
P. 98   Colonial Concept

CHAPTER 4 | The Unusual

P. 145   Sylvie Corbelin
P. 145   Isabelle Maleval
P. 150   Marta Bryl
P. 150   Lucas Ratton
P. 150   Patrick Ayme
P. 150   Yvan Devlay
P. 154   Pierre Bazalgues
P. 154   David Doussy

Appendix
P. 202   Geography of *les puces*
P. 204   Addresses
P. 207   Bibliography
P. 208   Credits and Acknowledgments

LES PUCES AT NIGHT
An aisle in the Serpette Market. For several days
each week, the antiques stay shuttered behind
the heavy metal curtains like Sleeping Beauties,
resting before their weekend show.

BIENVENUE

*A steel gate rattles noisily as it is thrown open. Then another. And another.
And so it goes, in an orchestrated rhythm. In the early morning, from aisle to aisle, from
market to market, the stalls come to life: The Saint-Ouen flea markets,
the largest in Paris, are setting up. Every weekend, in the rain, the wind, or under
a crushing sun, the flea markets once again open for business, an organized cacophony
of a well-calibrated ritual. Compulsive collectors, experienced bargain hunters,
bewildered tourists, timid first-timers, specialists in the one-of-a-kind item,
American designers, treasure seekers, Japanese fashionistas, anonymous celebrities,
decorators and designers looking for inspiration—each of them feels a rush
of adrenaline. Keep your eyes open. You might hit the jackpot!*

*This national treasure came into being in the late nineteenth century, grew and
flourished in the twentieth, and has endured ever since. This book is not intended
as an exhaustive guide to the Saint-Ouen flea markets but rather as a suggested
itinerary for a stroll, the chance to discover a unique spot in the world.
This book does not seek to reflect the reality so much as the mind-set of* les puces,
*as seen through the profiles of a few passionate antiques dealers and vendors
who want to pass on their life's knowledge.*

PAUL BERT MARKET
On a winter morning, an African statue braves the cold and snow.

MARCHÉ
PAUL BERT

Du 19 Mars au 2 Mai 2010

CARTE
BLANCHE
À ...

Stand 81 bis, Allée 6
Marché Paul Bert

CUISINE DE TRADITION
Service fait par des dames

LE PAUL

Café -

Du 19 Mars au 2 Mai 2010

CARTE
BLANCHE
À ...

Stand 81 bis, Allée 6
Marché Paul Bert

PAUL BERT MARKET
The entrance to the Paul Bert Market, the leading open-air
showcase for twentieth-century decorative arts.
Industrial furniture, art deco, the spirit of the 1930s,
the style of the 1940s, vintage Scandinavian design,
the revival of the 1970s...this is where new trends begin.

CHAPTER 1

JULES-VALLÈS MARKET
Antiques and objets d'art displayed at the stall
of the Frères Parent. Photograph by Luc Fournol.

HISTORY OF
LES PUCES

Welcome to a world unto itself: the planet's largest antiques market, spanning fifty acres. It has been thriving for 125 years. The official birth year of the flea markets was 1885, when village officials in Saint-Ouen took steps to codify the informal trade that had long been occurring. Their efforts included paving the streets, creating sidewalks, and requiring dealers to apply for permits before they could set up their stalls. But five years before, this area was still a Court of Miracles. Shady groups of rag-and-bone men, chased out of Paris, had settled in fields on the other side of the fortifications beyond the Porte de Clignancourt. These men, known as *biffins*, *chiftires*, or *crocheteurs* (because they combed through the rubbish with picks) or, more kindly, *pêcheurs de lune* (moon fishermen), roamed through the city at night, searching for odds and ends, scrap metal, and rags tossed into the trash, which they would resell the following morning in their improvised markets.

**LA PETITE SALLE À MANGER
(THE SMALL DINING ROOM)**
In the center of the Serpette Market, this tiny bar is the place to meet for small talk, bargaining, and deal-making.

(opposite) **CHEZ LOUISETTE**
Nestled at the far end of the Vernaison Market, this decades-old daytime cabaret, where La Môme Piaf used to perform, has retained all its authenticity.

THE ANTIQUES BUSINESS TAKES OFF

Around 1880, an anonymous bargain hunter coming across this teeming spectacle was said to have exclaimed, "My goodness, it's a flea market!" And so *les puces*—*puce* is French for "flea"—were born. The expression was coined immediately and even appeared on the first postcards showing the sights of the Porte de Clignancourt. In time, the activities of the markets gradually became more organized. Soon enough, the lure of the miscellaneous objects displayed directly on the ground by the rag-and-bone men, the *puciers*, attracted the first Parisians to the fairground shacks and open-air cafés. Then came the penniless artists of the Bateau Lavoir, led by Pablo Picasso, looking for old canvases that they

could reuse. Searching through the bric-a-brac for the rare gem was hard work. The process recalls these lines from Jacques Prévert's poem "Inventory":

One Louis the Fifteenth heel
One Louis the Sixteenth armchair
One Henry the Second sideboard two Henry the Third sideboards
　　　three Henry the Fourth sideboards
One odd drawer

As the number of visitors grew, so did the flea markets' purpose.

FROM THE VERNAISON MARKET TO THE BIRON MARKET, DEALERS FACE MANY DIFFICULTIES

Just as the curiosity merchants in Paris were earning a more respectable status as antiques dealers and setting up shop in *hôtels particuliers,* the dealers of Saint-Ouen opened their first stall market. The initiative was led by Romain Vernaison, who was in charge of space assignments at Les Halles, the central market of Paris, and the proprietor of a large area in Saint-Ouen, a triangle of land between the avenue Michelet, the rue des Rosiers, and the rue Voltaire. In 1920, the first tenants moved into the prefabricated wood barracks of the Vernaison Market. Soon thereafter, the Malik Market was established (7, rue Jules-Vallès), named for a world-weary Albanese prince. But life for the dealers was not easy. The village administration could be overzealous, demanding, among other things, that they take measures to clean up the area. The Biron Market (85, rue des Rosiers) opened in 1925, as a result of a rebellion by seventy dealers. These hard-liners set up their market on a parcel of land belonging to a Parisian jeweler (baptized "the Rosiers fields") and, thumbing their noses at the annoying bureaucracy, decided to exhibit only high-end merchandise. Gilt wood now had its own home here, a second Faubourg Saint-Honoré. But what makes these markets so special, so rich, is that everything is welcome. From antique silver to ordinary zinc, you can find it all at *les puces*. What's more, each object can be the start of a brand-new collection—or the find of a lifetime. How many second-rate paintings have become authentic works of art? A dream come true, for just a song.

SURREALISM FINDS AN ALLY: CONFORMISM IS ABANDONED

Well before social and cultural diversity became a fashionable political concept, it existed in Saint-Ouen. In the 1920s, the young Belgian guitarist Django Reinhardt, self-taught and exceptionally gifted, played his first chordal fills of Gypsy jazz in a rue des Rosiers bistro. The cabaret artist and renowned *argot* poet Aristide Bruant, the author of "Nini peau d'chien," pays homage to the *biffins,* the rag-and-bone men, in his song "À Saint-Ouen." A young singer performing Bruant's songs at the nearby restaurant Chez Louisette (aisle 10 of the Vernaison Market) was none other than the future Môme Piaf. Was it by chance or coincidence? A bit of the first, more of the second. The Saint-Ouen flea markets have always attracted the creative classes. They drew André Breton, for instance, who offers a very personal definition in *Nadja,* published in 1928:

I go there often, searching for objects that can be found nowhere else: old-fashioned, broken, useless, almost incomprehensible, even perverse—at least in the sense I give to the word and which I prefer—like, for example, that kind of irregular, white, shellacked half-cylinder covered with reliefs and depressions that are meaningless to me, streaked with horizontal and vertical reds and greens, preciously nestled in a case under a legend in Italian, which I brought home and which after careful examination I have finally identified as some kind of statistical device, operating three-dimensionally and recording the population of a city in such and such a year, though all this makes it no more comprehensible to me.

A mystery indeed. In *Mad Love* Breton recounts in great detail, a visit to Saint-Ouen with the Swiss sculptor Alberto Giacometti in the spring of 1934: "The objects that, between the lassitude of some and the desire of others, go off to dream at the antique fair had been just barely distinguishable from each other in the first hour of our stroll. [. . .]The first one of them that really attracted us, drawing us as something we had *never seen,* was a half-mask of metal, striking in its rigidity as well as in its forceful adaptation to a necessity unknown to us." Giacometti purchased it before Breton set his sights on "a large wooden spoon, of peasant fabrication but quite beautiful, it seemed to me, and rather daring in its form, whose handle, when it rested on its convex part, rose from a little shoe that was part of it."

This modest find would immediately become a catalyst. For that day, the great helmsman of surrealism was searching for an object he had long dreamed about: "a Cinderella ashtray." He had commissioned Giacometti to make one for him but, it seems, the sculptor was never inspired by the idea. Now Breton's wish had been fulfilled, thanks to a small wooden shoe discovered unexpectedly under the handle of the spoon. Many other objects from the Saint-Ouen flea markets must have played similar roles for Breton, based on those found in his Parisian apartment and eventually auctioned off at Drouot in April 2003, such as anthropomorphic pebbles, a frog-shaped snuffbox, Kabbalah medals, and molds for little wafers and cakes. The flea markets would play the part of a surrealist ally, slaying conformism and opening the door to the unconscious.

AN ENDLESS SOURCE OF INSPIRATION

Same time, same place: Two friends, who share the same first name and a bohemian spirit, wander through the flea markets. Christian Bérard was a young painter and a friend of Jean Cocteau's. He was also the companion of Boris Kochno, the Russian writer who was, at that time, the secretary to Sergei Diaghilev, the director of the Ballets Russes. Christian Dior had not yet become the designer of the New Look. Still disillusioned over an unrealized career as an architect, he had opened a contemporary art gallery on rue de la Boétie in Paris with his friend Jacques Bonjean. Times were difficult, but there were festive evenings to look forward to, for which they needed props and costumes. Kochno described how Bérard, or Bébé to his friends, "would wrap himself in a tablecloth and use an ice bucket as a headdress." The flea markets were a never-ending source of inspiration and supply. In *Villa Blanche,* a novel about the 1930s playwright Édouard Bourdet, Bruno Tessarech describes Kochno's style: "His interior design and costumes are immediately recognizable. He favors neoclassicism with torches, columns, Greek vases, flame finials, crystal chandeliers, giving them a new twist in Bérard's

CHRISTIAN BÉRARD
The French painter and designer (1902–49).

21

unpredictable color palette of pastel or acid hues. As for his costumes, they look like rags from *les puces* de Clignancourt, transformed by the artist's genius." Bérard, Dior, and their circle of friends, Max Jacob among them, happily shared curtains and lampshades among themselves.

MADELEINE CASTAING, THE "QUEEN OF *LES PUCES*"

They were not the only devotees. In his biography of Madeleine Castaing, Jean-Noël Liaut relates how

the designer, who had never been an early riser, liked to arrive at the Jules-Vallès market by eight o'clock in the morning. She would travel there on her bicycle, regardless of the weather, wearing one of her eccentric hats. At the time, that market was one of the most squalid in Saint-Ouen, a vast plot of land where only the most dedicated buyers would venture. The ground was covered with cinders to prevent people from sinking into the mud, and the hardiest among them often had to fight each other off to grab a particular treasure. Aging aristocratic Russian ladies, ruined by the Revolution, sold whatever they had managed to take with them before escaping their country, and the keen-eyed buyer could find real treasures at unbeatable prices inside these dismal wood barracks.

The quirky Castaing had such a sharp eye that it became her signature, a much sought-after style that was part Napoleon III, a pinch of Biedermeier and Regency, a soupçon of Directoire, and peppered with a few rustic Scandinavian pieces in unexpected colors, such as peacock blue, mint green, or pink. Many designers—from Jacques Grange to Jean-Louis Riccardi—still speak of the famous Castaing style in reverent tones. Caught up by the process of combing through the markets to furnish her *hôtel particulier* on the Left Bank, Castaing eventually opened her own shop at the Jules-Vallès Market: "Word of mouth immediately established the success of this woman with the extravagant hats who sold unusual pieces from the nineteenth century and who was known as the muse and patron of the great painter [Chaïm] Soutine. She quickly became the main attraction of the Jules-Vallès Market and was nicknamed 'the queen of *les puces*,'" writes Liaut. She was forty-five years old and would reign for many more years. Her disciples followed her in 1941 to her first boutique in the rue du Cherche-Midi, then in 1947 to her next location at the corner of rue Jacob and rue Bonaparte (occupied today by the famous *maison de patisserie* Ladurée).

MADELEINE CASTAING
(above)
The legendary antiques dealer in her Parisian shop on rue Jacob, 1985.
(opposite)
Madeleine Castaing's Paris home, in 1986.

A TIME OF FRIVOLITY FOR BÉRARD AND DIOR

The prewar frivolity had made a comeback, and 1947 was a very good year. The curious, the collectors, and the creative types returned once again to Clignancourt. Christian Bérard, who had become a well-known illustrator and costume designer for the theater, organized the Bal du Panache, "where every [sort of plume], from birds of paradise to ostrich to egret adorned the most beautiful heads in the world," recalled Christian Dior. After the success of his first fashion collection, Dior acquired the Moulin de Coudret, near Milly-la-Fôret. "I wanted my country house, my 'very own' house, to feel alive and 'lived-in.' And, despite the obligatory and given artifice of a rapid renovation, I was able to accomplish what I most desired: a sense of ease and of having been lived in for a long time." To achieve this, Dior combed through the flea markets.

THE BRIC-A-BRAC STYLE OF LOUISE DE VILMORIN

This fondness for time-weathered and seasoned pieces was shared by one of Dior's neighbors in the Essonne area, Louise de Vilmorin, whose Château de Verrières-le-Buisson was thirty miles from Coudret. Vilmorin was a poet and a novelist, but she was also an inveterate collector of tabletop objects and fine linens, as well as bear-shaped salt-shakers, chandeliers, and umbrella stands. She liked to say that "there is often nobody inside a person, but there is always somebody inside an object!" Jean Chalon, one of her close friends in the 1960s, recounts that Vilmorin, who was known for her generosity, would go to the flea markets at Christmastime to buy trinkets, baubles, and other little jewels, claiming, "In our family, we enjoy giving gifts."

(above)
LOUISE DE VILMORIN
Louise Leveque was her given name, and she was the muse of literary Paris. Every Saturday evening, she invited several creative types (such as Bernard Buffet, Max Ophüls, and Léo Férré) to dine at her Château de Verrières-le-Buisson. This photograph is from November 1968.

(opposite)
GABRIELLE "COCO" CHANEL
The French fashion designer (1883–1971) is pictured here in August 1937.

LUXURY ACCORDING TO CHANEL

This taste for bric-a-brac was completely foreign to Coco Chanel, though she also visited *les puces*. She especially enjoyed being recognized there after her successful comeback to couture in February 1954. "I accomplished something by reaching the top again. Now, people recognize me. When I go to the flea market, everyone says hello to me. They come and kiss me. I let them. It doesn't cost me anything, and it makes them happy, as Picasso used to say." There is, however, no record of what she may have bought. The extreme opposite of overabundance and showy luxury, Mademoiselle's style was discreet, almost ascetic. She did admit to a penchant for lacquer ("It's my element"), but she never divulged whether any of the thirty-two Coromandel lacquered screens she owned came from Saint-Ouen. "Me, I am like a snail. I carry my home with me," as she said. Never get attached to objects. Live at the Ritz as if it were a dormitory. Accumulate nothing.

THE EXUBERANCE OF RUDOLF NUREYEV

It was quite a different scenario for Rudolf Nureyev, a habitué of antiques stores in general and *les puces* in particular. Indeed, not all celebrities are alike. The nomadic dancer was a consumer, acquiring homes, rare objects, oriental textiles, antique furniture, and kilims. Ever since the extraordinary day in June 1961 at Le Bourget airport when he slipped past the KGB to choose liberty, he began shopping compulsively, perhaps to overcome or defy his sense of displacement. But Nureyev was also an aesthete: He liked to design sets, onstage and off. The opulent and colorful nineteenth century became his weakness just as exuberance was his style. His biographer Bertrand Meyer-Stabley describes how:

> *Nureyev, when he went to* les puces*, would sometimes send one of his friends into the shop before him to inquire about the cost, making sure that his celebrity did not inflate the price. He would wait a moment, then come inside and haggle like a rug sales-man; things could get so heated that his friends had been known to sneak away. Occasionally, to close the deal, he would address the dumbfounded dealer with tsar-worthy haughtiness: 'You do realize that I am Rudolf Nureyev?' He was often careful to spend no more than he would earn that very evening at a gala performance.*

DEALERS FIND THEIR CALLING

All are welcome at the flea markets, rich and poor alike. For very little money you can feast your eyes or cast your imagination into the future. How many dealers found their calling at the Clignancourt flea markets? One of the most illustrious was the late and greatly missed Jacques Kerchache, the man who first brought primitive art to the Louvre in 2000. Bravo! At the age of thirteen, Kerchache was already shopping at *les puces*, setting aside the best pieces for Max-Pol Fouchet, the writer, humanist, and television personality. Three years later, Kerchache had his first job running a gallery, the Iris Clert, on weekends. He then opened his own shop at 53, rue de Seine, where he introduced the works of Pol Bury, Carlos Cruz-Diez, Miodrag Djuric Dado, and Sam Szafran, before heading to Africa, Asia, and all the so-called primitive civilizations.

(above)
JACQUES KERCHACHE
The historian and collector
of African art, in Paris, 1986.

(opposite)
ANDY WARHOL
In a 1983 photograph
by Horst P. Horst.

However, the record for the most precocious career beginning belongs to Marc-Antoine Pâtissier, the owner of HP Le Studio on the Left Bank's rue Allent and an undisputed specialist in Italian rationalism from 1930 to 1950 and the architects and designers Franco Albini and Ignazio Gardella, among others. In 1971, when he was eight years old, he bought a Louis XV embroidered waistcoat from a dealer at the Paul Bert Market. He relates how his father was furious and promptly returned the "old rag," demanding full reimbursement of the eight hundred francs. Marc-Antoine thus suffered his first frustration as a bargain hunter. No hard feelings, though, as he eventually set up his own business in that very market with his faithful associate, Elisabeth Hervé.

(above)
RALPH KONNEMAN
Art et Design Gallery,
30, rue de Penthièvre, in Paris.

(opposite)
MARC ANTOINE PATISSIER
HP Le Studio
at 1, rue Allent, in Paris.

THE SPIRIT OF *LES PUCES*

Secondhand dealers are also pioneers. Saint-Ouen can derive much pride from the fact that fifteen hundred dealers and no less than sixteen markets, not to mention all the shops in the adjacent streets, share in the good fortune of flea-market shopping. Discover the low-key Jules-Vallès Market with its two hairpin-shaped aisles. It was opened in 1938 by Amedeo Cesana, a Venetian, and was the first covered market. Wander through the Malassis Market, established in 1989; the Dauphine Market, famous for its Bookshop Square; or the previously mentioned Vernaison and Biron markets. Head to the Entrepôt market for oversize pieces, such as garden pavilions, castle gates, and wood paneling from stately homes. And don't forget the celebrated and linked Paul Bert and Serpette markets. The Paul Bert—an open-air market named after the French physiologist and politician who, with Jules Ferry, founded secular schools—was established in 1946 on land owned by the son of a market gardener, Louis Poré. The site of the Serpette Market was previously a Citroën garage, bought in 1970 by Alain Serpette, a dealer who specialized in antique weapons. Always at the forefront of new trends, these two markets are responsible for many rediscoveries in the field of decorative arts of the twentieth century.

The spirit of *les puces* burns like an eternal flame. The spirit of *les puces* is hope in all its forms. The spirit of *les puces* is a way of life.

CHAPTER 2

THE

CLASSIC

While the traditional dealers do not generate the most buzz at the Saint-Ouen flea markets, they are the ones who are timeless. They were there before the fads and trends appeared and will remain long after. They represent the true spirit of les puces.

MARIANNE AND ALBERT RODRIGUEZ

15, rue Jules-Vallès

The rue Jules-Vallès has been the domain of Marianne and Albert Rodriguez, one of the most engaging couples at *les puces* since 1977, "from dawn to dusk, January to December." Starting out "on the sidewalks," as they describe it, the couple now occupies a space measuring ten thousand square feet (15, rue Jules-Vallès), where they deal primarily in antiques from the nineteenth century—cabinets, ceramics, chairs, chests, lanterns, entire living rooms—all of it laid out in a happy muddle alongside commanding decorative elements, mainly wood paneling. Marianne and Albert would never consider moving. The sense of freedom at *les puces* is too appealing.

LÉON BENAÏM

97, rue des Rosiers

Léon Benaïm is one of the other *personalités* of *les puces*, a fixture for the past forty years. From the flea markets in Casablanca, where, he says, "I always liked things that did not sell," to his spot at 97, rue des Rosiers, "after a stop at each of the Saint-Ouen markets," Monsieur Léon, as he is called, eventually decided to specialize in the eighteenth century. Over the years, he fell in love with that period and has sold museum-quality signed pieces by the most eminent cabinetmakers of the time, including Jean-Henri Reisener, Jean-François Oeben, Bernard Molitor, Adam Weisweiler, BVRB (Bernard Van Risenburgh),

DIDIER THIERY
PAUL BERT MARKET
AISLE 2, STALL 117
Works on paper are everywhere—from the top of the wall moldings to the floor, stacks upon stacks. Watch your step!

33

and Nicolas Petit. "Every time," he says, "you just get lucky and find it! From nowhere!" Benaïm's holy grail? A fountain belonging to Joachim Murat, the brother-in law of Napoleon I and the King of Naples, made of multitoned porphyry. Benaïm has passed on his love of collecting to his daughter, who has a stall at the Biron Market.

JANE AND NICHOLAS MOUFFLET
Biron Market, aisle 1, stall 1

The passion of collecting can be hereditary—passed from mother to son this time, and also in the Biron Market. Jane and Nicholas Moufflet specialize in posters and original prints from the Belle Époque through 1935, such as *The Four Seasons* by Alphonse Mucha, various posters of Aristide Bruant by Henri de Toulouse-Lautrec, the well-known poster by Adolphe Mouron Cassandre of the steamship *Normandie*, other prominent works by Jean Carlu, Paul Colin, Hervé Morvan, Raymond Savignac, and Bernard Villemot, and in a corner, a striking abstract poster from 1989 by Roy Lichtenstein for the eightieth anniversary of the American Federation of Arts, signed by the artist.

FRANÇOISE-ANNE AND FRANÇOIS BACHELIER
Paul Bert Market, aisle 1, stall 17

Françoise-Anne and François Bachelier, another dynamic mother-and-son team located at the Paul Bert Market, specialize in kitchenware, such as copper pots and kitchen utensils, pottery, and baskets. Their cheerful approach extends beyond their shop. Françoise-Anne has written a cookbook (*Toqués de terrines*, or, roughly, *Hooray for Pâté*), and every two years, they organize a contest for the best pâté. Contestants come from as far away as Japan and Australia. On the night the award is bestowed, their shop overflows with people—the winners, the judges, supporters, friends, and fellow dealers, a diverse little world that is a microcosm of *les puces*.

HENRI AND LAURENCE VEYRIER
Librairie de l'Avenue, 31, rue Lecuyer

Henri and Laurence Veyrier, father and daughter, own a shop worthy of the record books. Sixty-five hundred square feet of selling space with an equal amount of storage, with more than half a mile of shelves and more than 150,000 volumes make up their bookstore, the Librairie de l'Avenue. Founded in 1961, within its walls are many treasures, including the first French edition of James Cook's voyages, a large nineteenth-century herbarium, a book about Salvador Dalí with an original drawing by the artist, another about Marc Chagall that also features an original drawing, as well as myriad other books, new and old,

MARIE GERONIMI
Marie Geronimi (mariegeronimi@wanadoo.fr), a fixture at the Serpette Market for twenty-five years, is known for her love of both decorating and travel.
(opposite)
A celebration of Italy: an eighteenth-century console from Tuscany, made of wood imitating stone, and a Florentine mirror from the early nineteenth-century; a neo-Gothic (circa 1850) chandelier; and curved glass wall sconces and table lamps in silver-plated metal, early twentieth century.
(preceding pages)
A nineteenth-century English display case in lacquered steel, a pair of Roman pots in cast iron, Sergio Rodriguez–style chairs made of wood and leather from the twentieth century, and an Austrian ceiling light in the manner of the Weiner Werkstätte.

(following pages)
CLAUDE-ANNIE MARZET
SERPETTE MARKET
Claude-Annie Marzet (marzet.expert@gmail.com) is an expert advisor for the CEA (Compagnie d'expertise en antiquités et objets d'art). She has spent many years at *les puces*, first at the Biron Market, and now at the Serpette Market. Under the lights of several Murano glass chandeliers, a dog-umbrella stand and a screen by Fornasetti (circa 1950); on either side, two American chairs (circa 1970) and two chairs from Brazil (circa 1980).

waiting to enlighten enthusiasts on any subject from Cistercian art to Ciceronian humanism, with a detour to elementary geometry.

JANINE GIOVANNONI

Vernaison Market, aisles 3 and 7, stall 141

Objects do not always require a specific seal or brand to be considered classic; they can simply be appealing—such as the colorful linens dating from 1930 to 1950 featured by Janine Giovannoni at the Vernaison Market. She is so trusted that her clients buy sheets, tablecloths, and other linens "without even unfolding them." Explains Giovannoni, "Whether they are made of hemp or silk, their quality holds up over time." Lace, embroidery, or more pedestrian textiles, from breathtaking draperies to modest handkerchiefs, there is no shortage of choices at this lovely shop.

PATRICK MORCOS

Serpette Market, aisle 4, stalls 23 and 24

A classic item can take many forms, as seen in the stand overseen by Patrick Morcos in the Serpette Market. A self-described "expert in unusual items from 2000 B.C. to 2000 A.D.," this lively dealer chose to be a generalist so that he would never have to "hold back." Choose from a field officer's candleholder from the eighteenth century, a cachepot from the Ottoman Empire made of hammered brass, lamps from the 1970s, a nineteenth-century boat model, antique sculpture from the same period, or a painting depicting ancient ruins in the style of the Grand Tour—classic perhaps, but never boring.

LA MAISON JAMES

Vernaison Market, aisle 1, stalls 49, 50, and 51, and aisle 10, stall 247
Serpette Market, aisle 4, stalls 20 and 21

Because of the timelessness of their goods, these dealers of classic merchandise have been around for generations. Maison James, established in 1912, is such an example. The family started out as coffee traders from the north who settled in Saint-Ouen in the early days of *les puces*. They eventually began to dabble in secondhand trading, selling small furnishings. Little by little, they refined their selections: "We went up in style," as they say. Today, Maison James occupies three separate locations, two in the Vernaison Market and one in the Serpette. The third generation of the James family now sells European antiques from the seventeenth, eighteenth, and nineteenth centuries. Their shops are little museums, small replicas of beautiful homes, filled with Empire-style desks, period canopy beds (*lits à la polonaise*), crystal chandeliers, parquetry flooring, and small clocks to turn back time.

(opposite)
RÉMY LABERGERE AND VINCENT VAUBAN
PAUL BERT MARKET
AISLE 1, STALL 142
A mix of styles by Emilio Terry and Charles de Beistegui: an oak bureau from 1940, Napoleon III–era velvet chairs, a sun mirror, a pair of small bronze obelisks, a 1970 Roseaux lamp from the Maison Charles. Not quite the Château de Groussay, but almost!

(following pages)
STÉPHANE OLIVIER
LA PETITE MAISON,
10 RUE PAUL BERT
Doric columns of stone become steles; lion-head masks serve as lamp bases. Olivier favors traditional furnishings, naturalist objects, and the look that comes from the patina of time. A mercury glass mirror, antique plaster figures, delicate white corals set in trophy-like bases—all these can be found between the courtyard and the garden of his Petite Maison, where yesterday's objects curios are offered for today's pleasure.

HUGUETTE PORTEFAIX

Biron Market, aisle 1, stall 121

Even the decorative arts of the early twentieth century are now considered classics. Art nouveau is the specialty of Huguette Portefaix in the Biron Market. She features glasswork that was very much in demand, pieces signed by Daum, François Décorchemont, Émile Gallé, or Almeric Walter and made of colored glass decorated with floral or animal motifs. Other pieces, such as those by Gabriel Argy-Rousseau, have more of a neoclassic feel. One beautiful vase of white *pâte de verre,* featuring three dancers inside blue flower medallions, blends classicism, femininity, and poetry. A passionate glassworks expert, Portefaix also showcases pieces from the period between 1930 and 1950, such as geometric patterned vases by Jean Luce and André Thuret's monochrome glass vases with touched with gold—classicism, elegance, and modernity.

MARTINE VALLI, PAUL BERT MARKET, AISLE 3, STALL 149
Industrial design had its first success at Saint-Ouen. Enthusiasts celebrated both its functional scale and simplicity.

(following pages)
CHRISTIAN LECLERC, PAUL BERT MARKET, AISLE 3, STALL 280
A Napoleon III pedestal table, neoclassical engravings of antique statuary, a Gustavian style chair, a Swedish console, a horse from a merry-go-round, cast-iron Medici vases and screens decorated with portraits in the style of Goya...
This charming stall is full of treasures from the eighteenth and nineteenth centuries.

BRUNO LANGLOIS, PAUL BERT MARKET, AISLE 4, STALL 215
(above) A selection of antiques, including a Napoleon III–era sofa, a nineteenth-century bureau, an oil lamp, a pair of Directoire-style *cassolettes* made of lacquered metalware, and a late-nineteenth-century bust of Molière.
(opposite) A florist's table, a painted trumeau, assorted fabrics, shutters that have been turned into screens—this dealer has a particular fondness for utilitarian furniture and the patina of the nineteenth century. In the foreground, 1950s ceramic cups from the Cérenne atelier in Vallauris, France.

GÉRARD MIZEL, SERPETTE MARKET, AISLE 1, STALL 41
A crystal chandelier, a Murano glass chandelier, lanterns; two chandeliers, one in crystal, the other in Murano glass; precariously balanced neo-Egyptian stools, painted wood vases with chinoiserie decor; and a foot belonging to a centurion, a legionnaire, or even a Roman emperor—it's anyone's guess, but it's impressive!

(preceding pages)
(left)
LAURENCE VAUCLAIR, AIDJOLATE, PAUL BERT MARKET, AISLE 6, STALL 79
This "house filled with joy" (the meaning of *aidjolate* in the Swiss dialect of the Jura Mountains) is not to be missed. These two happy figurines made of barbotine ware (Eichwald, nineteenth century, Austria) seem to agree.
On either side: large iron lamps from the 1950s and two nineteenth-century Italian neo-Gothic chairs with ivory inlay.
(right)
ELSA HALFEN AND CLÉMENT ROSENZWEIG, PAUL BERT MARKET, AISLE 2, STALL 121
A beautiful display of several painters' palettes, a zinc statue of a bird, and a nineteenth-century worktable with drawers. The chairs are from the era of Napoleon III.

BENOÎT FAUQUENOT, OLIVIER D'YTHURBIDE AND ASSOCIÉ, SERPETTE MARKET, AISLE 6, STALL 25
What could this lovely woman, dressed in the fashion of the eighteenth century, be dreaming about?
She is eternally poised, remaining serene as countless visitors walk by. She is almost too elegant for her noisy surroundings.
At *les puces,* you must always be alert: The finest object is not always the first one you see.

(preceding pages)
(left)
GILLES DÉRIOT, SERPETTE MARKET, AISLE 1, STALL 37
Le classique, c'est chic! A small bucking horse in porcelain from Vienna (early twentieth century) standing on a half-moon-shaped walnut console
(south-east France, late eighteenth century). On the wall, a painting of peonies on silk (part of a nineteenth-century Japanese screen)
as well as a pair of French engravings (second half of the eighteenth century).
(right)
MARTA BRYL, KERAMION, SERPETTE MARKET, AISLE 1, STALL 16
This specialist in antiquities has a soft spot for black-figured Greek ceramics, lekythos, and other kraters embellished with colonettes.
Many other interesting objets d'art can be found here, including Etruscan or Roman pieces, as well as those from the Renaissance;
all are inspired by the ancient world.

THIERRY FERRAND, PAUL BERT MARKET, AISLE 4, STALL 203
Corner pieces in lacquered wood from the late eighteenth century; a very rare example of cement outdoor furniture (circa 1880);
and a Louis XVI–era chair stamped by Lebas. On the wall, a tapestry from the seventeenth-century Brussels ateliers provides a background of greenery.

(following pages)
At first glance, these picture frames of gilded wood and this elegant divinity from Asia would seem an unlikely pairing—yet in the magical universe of
les puces, styles can mix wonderfully. The same applies to the antique dealers and collectors who, each week, fill the busy aisles of all the markets.

DIDIER THIERY, PAUL BERT MARKET, AISLE 2, STALL 117
Ah, memories…This dealer has set his sights on civilian historical objects "from Waterloo to Sedan" from 1815 to 1870: paintings, busts, tableware, and linens that perhaps belonged to French sovereigns of the nineteenth century.

(above) **PASCAL WEITZ, ABC PASCAL, PAUL BERT MARKET, AISLE 1, STALL 63**
A joyous mix of gilded and painted wood. Also, a wonderful selection of mirrors: convex, Empire, sun-shaped, and Venetian.
Mirror, mirror on the wall…

(opposite) **DIDIER THIÉRY, PAUL BERT MARKET, AISLE 2, STALL 117**
This is the meeting place for those who are passionate about both history and beautiful objects. The Empire is within reach,
as if Napoleon and the beautiful Josephine had just stopped by for tea.

CAROLE AND PASCAL LEMOINE, LA MAISON DU ROY, SERPETTE MARKET, AISLE 5, STALLS 1 AND 2
(opposite) A selection of woodwork, columns and stands, terra-cotta busts, chairs and armchairs, portraits, and paintings of *scènes galantes*—
everything one needs for château living.
(following pages, right) These antiques dealers set the boudoir mood with furniture, paintings, and objets d'art dating mostly from the eighteenth century.

(following pages, left) **THIBAULT NOSSEREAU, PAUL BERT MARKET, AISLE 3, STALL 159**
Yesterday's functional pieces, such as this vintage postal sorting desk with many compartments, have a bright future.

CAROLE AND PASCAL LEMOINE, LA MAISON DU ROY, SERPETTE MARKET, AISLE 5, STALLS 1 AND 2
Commedia dell'arte atmosphere in the eighteenth century: a Louis XV–era bureau and a *robe à la française* from the 1760s.
A copy of Watteau's famous painting *Embarquement pour Cythère* (France, circa 1750) forms the backdrop.

(following pages)
(left)
PATRICK MORCOS, SERPETTE MARKET, AISLE 4, STALL 23
An eighteenth-century stone head of a Chinese divinity, a gouache of flowers on nineteenth-century vellum paper,
a twentieth-century plaster head by Robert Muller—all excellent choices.
(right)
Nostalgia, the patina of time, a provenance from long ago, an exotic source...
Even when an object is of unknown origin, it has a "voice," a story, an intrinsic value, beyond that of any monetary value.

VIRGILE WAHL-BOYER, PAUL BERT MARKET, AISLE 4, STALL 148

A fragment of a white marble column from Roman times; a seated Buddha from the ancient kingdom of Siam (Sukhotai period, sixteenth century), a pair of iron andirons that belonged to paleographer Henry-René d'Allemagne, a galvanized bust of Henri IV copied from a Louis XIV– era original, a large painted trumeau from the late eighteenth century, inlaid wood frames (Eastern Europe, 1913), a Mumuye statue from Nigeria (circa 1920), a Miao theater mask (China, circa 1930)… This very young dealer already has great taste!

(following pages)

PATRICK MORCOS, SERPETTE MARKET, AISLE 4, STALL 23

A perfect representation of *les puces*: total eclecticism. A profusion of paintings and objets d'art dating from the end of the sixteenth century to 1900, among them a seventeenth-century French pietà made of wood; a nineteenth-century French marble vase mounted on bronze; a nineteenth-century German jasper goblet to be used as a decanter; and a nineteenth-century painting of the Grand Tour depicting antique ruins.

FATMIR TARAJ, PAUL BERT MARKET, AISLE 1, STALL 19
A clock and oversize printer's letters; chandeliers with or without drops; dishes, baskets, mirrors, and other decorative items—popular artifacts in a country atmosphere.

MICHÈLE PERCEVAL, SERPETTE MARKET, AISLE 5, STALL 26
Statues made of stone, metal chandeliers, credenzas, and paneling. In the spirit of *les puces*, antique materials and decorative elements coexist perfectly, far from their places of origin and headed for new destinations.

(above) **LAURENCE VAUCLAIR, AIDJOLATE, PAUL BERT MARKET, AISLE 1, STALL 77**
Sometimes an object will catch your eye—and stop you in your tracks. A moment of grace within a world of commotion:
an antique ceramic vase adorned with winged putti.
(opposite) **MARC CARLOTTO, PAUL BERT MARKET, AISLE 4, STALL 209**
A selection of lamps from the last two centuries, works on paper, and several pieces of furniture—all enchanting objects.

CHAPTER 3

THE
MODERN

The flea markets have always been a place for open-air improvisation, where young dealers with great flair and small means rekindle a taste for abandoned objects.

This long and successful story began in the 1960s with the rediscovery of art nouveau, followed by art deco. Be bold, invest in Émile Gallé, take a chance on Jacques-Émile Ruhlmann, take your winnings and start over quickly—before the established dealers and interior designers (American or otherwise) move in and push the prices out of reach. No more Eileen Gray, Pierre Legrain, Jean-Charles Moreux; many of these design pieces were dispersed following the 1972 sale of the estate of Jacques Doucet, the fashion designer and patron of the arts. There was no shortage of interested buyers. The artists of the 1940s, such as André Arbus, Marc du Plantier, Gilbert Poillerat, and Serge Roche, provided many new opportunities: "You could pick up a Jean-Michel Frank for almost nothing," remembers Alexandre Biaggi, the Parisian antiques dealer. Since then, he says, the prices have "many more zeros at the end." These decorative pieces of furniture that once elicited contempt have now become collector's items.

Because of their rarity, these pieces eventually disappeared from the flea markets altogether. However, the connection between antiques and interior design has remained. More and more, antiques dealers stage their displays, especially at the Paul Bert Market. Since 1980, and thanks to the talent of dealers such as Christian Sapet, the Paul Bert has become the mecca of twentieth-century decorative arts. Serge Mouille, Alexandre Noll, Charlotte Perriand, Jean Prouvé, Jean Royère—this dream cast ensured the fame of the future 1950s specialists such as Philippe Jousse, Jacques Lacoste, François Laffanour, and Patrick Seguin. But again, as prices began to soar, some dealers had to change direction.

MARIE AND CYRIL GRIZOT
Paul Bert Market, aisle 5, stalls 216 and 218

Known for their reliability and curiosity, Marie and Cyril Grizot are among the old-timers. Theirs is a tasteful mix of Roger Capron ceramics, Pierre Guariche lamps, Jean Lurçat tapestries, and Mathieu Matégot

PASCAL CUISINIER
PAUL BERT MARKET
AISLE 6, STALL 91
A chandelier by set designer and theater director Jean-Pierre Vincent, a pair of lamps by Pierre Disderot, a coffee table by Joseph-André Motte, a ceramic panel by Jacques Pouchain, and a cabinet by Roger Landault—Cuisinier, an avid researcher, specializes in the 1950s.

urniture. All in all, "objects that did well in their categories." Then, about fifteen years ago, they rediscovered the works of Yonel Lebovici. Taking a cue from Marcel Duchamp, this sculptor and designer transformed objects (a giant trombone, a little spaceship, an oversize electric plug, a satellite, to name a few) and created some of the most unusual lamps of the 1970s and '80s.

GUILHEM FAGET

Serpette Market, aisle 6, stall 9

With the same conviction as the Grizots, the thirty-year-old Guilhem Faget champions "unrecognized" artists of the 1970s, among them Philippe Cheverny, Philippe Jean, and Paul Legeard. "I am constantly refining my selections," he says. Inside Faget's shop, one finds a few splashes of color with Gabriella Crespi's photograph stands and a touch of couture with brushed-steel-and-black-velvet chairs from Pierre Cardin Décoration, as well as "a few surprises" hung on the walls, including contemporary works of art, photographs by Raphaël Dautigny, and paintings by Damien Bestieu.

PASCAL CUISINIER

Paul Bert Market, aisle 6, stall 91

Instinct, patience, and knowledge are the requirements for any serious dealer. Pascal Cuisinier, who has a degree in architecture and a PhD in the philosophy of art, promotes the top French designers of the 1950s: Janine Abraham, André Monpoix, Alain Richard, Olivier Mourgue, Michel Mortier, and Joseph-André Motte, as well as renowned lamp creators of the time, such as Jacques Biny and Pierre Disderot. Twice a year, Cuisinier organizes a show in his stall of a single designer's works, requiring months—if not years—of research and warehousing. His next show is devoted to the works of Meuble TV (for "Tricoire" and "Vecchione," not an abbreviation for "television"), a furniture company that was at its peak in the 1950s and '60s.

RAPHAËL DRUET

Paul Bert Market, aisle 1, stall 136

The twentieth century may have only lasted one hundred years, but it spawned an extraordinary multitude of styles around the world: lamps by Gino Sarfatti in Italy; chairs by Charles Eames and desks by George Nelson in the United States; Ado Chale tables from Belgium; and all kinds of designs from the Scandinavian countries (predominantly Denmark and Sweden), which have maintained their esteemed reputation. Raphaël Druet says he was a serious collector for more than ten years before "jumping to the other side" and opening a stall at the Paul Bert Market entirely devoted to Scandinavian designs. "What

**SERPETTE MARKET
AISLE 5, STALL 19**
Ava Gardner, draped in leopard, shows off her beautiful legs atop a nest of tables.

(preceding pages)
**RAPHAËL DRUET
PAUL BERT MARKET,
AISLE 1, STALL 138**
"Pentagon" armchair by Hans Haugaard (back left); "Hunting chair" by Borge Mogensen (back right); "Laminex chair" by Jens Nielsen (front, right); a metal chrome fixture, a cabinet, and a teak coffee table—this dealer specializes in Scandinavian design from 1950 to 1970. Nobody is excluded: Unknown and unrecognized designers such as Peter Hvidt and Orla Molgaard Nielsen are shown alongside the most famous, including Finn Juhl, Poul Kjaerholm, and Hans Wegner.

I like about Scandinavian style is that the material is straightforward. The furniture is always made according to precise specifications. On the other hand, I do not like *le total look* "of unleavened asceticism, Druet says. He does not hesitate to mix Bruno Mathsson–style chairs with a rare wood-and-wicker worktable by Hans Wegner and a sixteenth-century Dutch religious painting. Through his efforts, Druet brought to the forefront artists such as Peter Hvidt and Orla Molgaard Nielsen, who were not as well known as Arne Jacobsen, Finn Juhl, and Poul Kjaerholm.

GILLES OUDIN
Paul Bert Market, aisle 7, stall 405

Names, names, so many names. Yet there were other categories, such as industrial artifacts from 1880 to 1950, that did not require a designer's name. An expert in that field is Gilles Oudin, who has been a fixture at *les puces* for twenty years, following four years in which he divided his time between Saint-Ouen and a gallery in Paris. Oudin sells architects' tables, industrial chairs, ingeniously articulated lamps (by Bernard-Albin Gras, Jieldé, or anonymous artists), and oversize cabinets. Because they originally had a function, every piece of furniture is clever, timeless, and without embellishment. Still, there is the occasional unusual item. Oudin remembers a collection of nineteenth-century Dutch cranes, miniature models, reduced to the tenth degree, that were used as samples for professional trade shows.

YANN GUÉRIN
Vernaison Market, aisle 8, stall 167

Yann Guérin believes in the twentieth century, "for young people, students, and an atmosphere of fun." For that very reason, after twenty years in business, in 2009, when he was about to turn forty, he moved to the Vernaison Market. His stall is fun and friendly, with carpeting and camouflage wall coverings. There you can find 1950s coffee tables by Jacques Tournus; easy chairs from the same period by Pierre Gautier-Delaye; a 1970 armoire by Marc Berthier, made for the popular French cheap-chic chain Prisunic; a 1980 modular étagère by Ecart International; as well as Hell's Angels–style leather jackets draped over Harry Bertoia chairs, and a large collection of sunglasses—just a few examples of how this seasoned dealer successfully blends design and collectibles.

MARIE-LAURE DAVEAU-QUEYSANNE AND DIDIER ROYER, PAUL BERT MARKET, AISLE 2, STALL 127
These antiques dealers have furnished their stall with a spectacular "Living Wall" of oxidized and hammered copper (1969) by Pierre Sabatier. Other artists whose work is featured here: Juan Romero and his sculpture in black galalith (circa 1940); and Christel Sadde, whose 2010 golden mobile illuminates the ceiling.

NICOLAS GIOVANNONI
Serpette Market, aisle 6, stalls 8 and 10

Design, and furniture design in particular, doesn't have a monopoly on modernity. Other types of objects, such as tableware, can offer many surprises, especially in the hands of Nicolas Giovannoni. For more than

twenty years, first at the Vernaison Market and now at Serpette since 1991, Giovanonni's weekend offerings might include crystal glasses, sets of porcelain or faience dishes, and opaline *bonbonnières*. His inventory is always limited: "I like to work under pressure," he says. Giovanonni is not locked into any particular time period. From the early nineteenth century to the 1970s or '80s, he is always searching for the atypical object rather than the conventional one. He admits an attraction to art deco works by Marcel Goupy or Jean Luce—pieces that are "sober, elegant, devoid of ostentation." Before buying his first set of dishes, Giovannoni sold vintage rock-and-roll records and earned a law degree. He occupies a stall that belonged to Clara Scremini, the eponymous owner of a famed contemporary ceramics and glass gallery in Paris. Apparently, success begets success.

LA PETITE MAISON

10, rue Paul Bert

Spurred on by Christian Sapet, who once had a small shop in aisle 6 of the Paul Bert Market, the modern dealers have become talented stage directors. The difference between antiques dealers and interior designers is now almost negligible. Situated at 10, rue Paul Bert, La Petite Maison is anything but petite. Welcome to a world that encompasses both naturalism and the fantastic, as envisioned by Stéphane Olivier, a man who is passionate about garden decor. His period pieces include cast-iron flower pots from the mid–nineteenth century, early-twentieth-century garden furniture made of cement but resembling wood, old-style statuary, cast-iron enameled chairs from Northern Europe, stuffed birds, strange objects that could be Masonic, and frames made of seashells—a fascinating universe poised somewhere between the visions of Janine Janet and Emilio Terry.

COLONIAL CONCEPT

8, rue Paul Bert

A little further along, at 8, rue Paul Bert, another astonishing voyage begins when you step into Colonial Concept. Welcome to exoticism! Can Pierre Loti be very far? You are in the realm of the antiques dealer and interior designer François Daneck. As you walk through a garden filled with palm and banana trees, a jungle of eye-catching furniture and objects awaits you: stuffed animals, corals, Native American headdresses, Zulu hats, fossils, primitive masks and statues, and accent furniture covered in—of course—animal skins.

(opposite)
LISETTE AND HENRI SCHWEIZER-HOERNI PAUL BERT MARKET AISLE 4, STALL 217
A look of elegance and sobriety: a Danish credenza and a chandelier from the 1960s; a grouping of glass and ceramic vases from the 1940s from Biot, Daum, and Boch Frères Kéramis.

(following pages)
MARC-OLIVIER HESSE PAUL BERT MARKET AISLE 1, STALL 35
An extraordinary pair of 1930s crackle glaze ceramic vases made by the Frères Mougin of the Ecole de Nancy, placed on a 1940s Strafor industrial shelf.

ELIZABETH LECLERC, PAUL BERT MARKET, AISLE 4, STALL 223
A marble bust signed by Rossi, dated 1942; a piece of 1940s Cuban furniture made of black wood and mahogany, in the style of Jules Leleu; a door of cutout metal—this dealer specializes in elegant antiques.

(above) **STALL 97, PAUL BERT MARKET, AISLE 6, STALLS 95-97**
This spectacular mirror of painted and gilded wood (twentieth century) makes a big statement! A coffee table in travertine and plaster (circa 1940),
an iron dental instrument cabinet (circa 1950) and a pair of lamps by Marie Brem (twentieth century).

(opposite) **STÉPHANE ECOURTEMER, ARTOCARPUS, PAUL BERT MARKET, AISLE 4, STALL 211 BIS**
This stall gives prominent placement to French and Scandinavian tableware from 1950 to 1970, and to twentieth-century
furniture. Shown here, a beautiful selection of French ceramics from the 1950s created by Gilbert Valentin (of the studio Les Archanges),
Robert Picault, Jacques Ruelland, and Roger Capron, as well as Pablo Picasso and the Madoura atelier.

(above and opposite)
FRÉDÉRIC BORDES, ARNAUD DUCHESNE, SOPHIE MONTABERT, AND PHILIPPE ROLDAN, PAUL BERT MARKET, 5, IMPASSE SIMON
Here the style of the 1970s flirts with that of the '80s. The Italian sofa by de Sede, the mural sculpture by Pierre Sabatier,
the painting by Gérard Schlosser, the lamp by Philippe Jean, and the totem columns by Guy de Rougemont belong to the '70s.
The carpet, by Elizabeth Garouste and Mattia Bonetti, is from the '80s.

PAUL BERT MARKET, AISLE 4, STALL 172
Les puces are a world in constant flux, allowing vendors and the most audacious antiques dealers the freedom to stage almost any short-lived scene. Industrial style, primitive statuary, objects of natural science… every dealer has the opportunity to present his or her passion of the moment!

(preceding pages)
(left)
RÉMY LABERGERE AND VINCENT VAUBAN, PAUL BERT MARKET, AISLE 1, STALL 142
Lighted wall mirrors from the 1970s, paintings by Jean-Pierre Le Boul'ch from 1991, a collection of early-nineteenth-century ceramic vases displayed on a walnut cabinet—a lovely example of eclecticism.
(right)
STALL 97, PAUL BERT-MARKET, AISLE 6, STALLS 95-97
Shades of sunny yellow reign, thanks to two fiberglass and lacquered resin chairs by Dominique Prévot (France Design, 1970).
Sunburst mirror in painted and gilded wood, twentieth century.

(above and opposite)

KATIA APELBAUM AND ARNAUD VOLFINGER, SERPETTE MARKET, AISLE 3, STALL 23

Sixties-era Scandinavian designs—a Kurt Ostervig desk made of Brazilian rosewood, a Finn Juhl chair, glass objects from the Holmegaard factory—are prominently displayed in a spare and uncluttered setting. On the wall are silk screens by the French artist Auguste Herbin.

ERIC FLEURET, PAUL BERT MARKET, AISLE 5, STALL 212
Vibrant colors and dashing lines: a tour de force of 1950s design. Furniture by Cees Braakman, Florence Knoll, and Coen de Vries; lamps by Verner Panton, Joe Hammerborg, and Wim Rietveld.

(preceding pages)
(left)
BENJAMIN BAILLON, PAUL BERT MARKET, AISLE 2, STALL 143 AND SERPETTE MARKET, AISLE 6, STALLS 16 AND 17
Arne Jacobsen chairs (circa 1960s), photographs of flowers by Cédric Porchez (2008), plaster head from the 1940s and ceramic masks (Italy, 1970s) resting on an oak credenza from 1910.
(right)
NATHALIE WILSON AND OLIVIER FRANQUET, PAUL BERT MARKET, AISLE 3, STALL 157
Nostalgia and contrast are evoked here: utilitarian school desks and a masterpiece of 1950s design, the Tulip chair, by Eero Saarinen.

(above) **MARIE-LAURE DAVEAU-QUEYSANNE AND DIDIER ROYER, PAUL BERT MARKET, AISLE 2, STALL 127**
The resin "Wall of Light" (circa 1960–70) by François and Marie Chapuis; a pair of 1960 English chairs in the style of the eighteenth century;
a group of pastel paintings of African masks from 1960; and a 2010 Christel Sadde mobile—eclecticism reigns at *les puces*.

(opposite) **FRÉDÉRIC BORDES, ARNAUD DUCHESNE, SOPHIE MONTABERT, AND PHILIPPE ROLDAN, PAUL BERT MARKET, 5, IMPASSE SIMON**
A Maurice Calka sculpture and a standing lamp made of fractal resin—an example of 1970s originality.

FRANÇOIS DE BAYSER, PAUL BERT MARKET, AISLE 4, STALL 152
An ink portrait by Henri de Waroquier (1937); *Nu bleu no. 5*, an oil painting by Jun Dobashi (circa 1970); a drawing by Liuba (1967); terra-cotta and plaster sculptures by Hélène Guastalla (circa 1940–1950) … a selection of objects that combine rigor and sensibility.

KARINE SZANTO, SERPETTE MARKET, AISLE 6, STALL 14
Square wall lights of stainless steel and chromed metal; black lacquer side lamps by Jean-Claude Mahé; a polished nickel standing lamp
with a rectangular base by the Maison Barbier; an Oded Chamir sculpture in black-and-white marble; a black melamine and steel round coffee table
by Willy Rizzo; a rare bucrane in cast aluminum—Szanto shows off the full 1970s look.

(following pages)
(left)
JEAN-MARC JAGER, SERPETTE MARKET, AISLE 6, STALL 12
Fiat Lux! (Let there be light!) Lamps and lighting fixtures from the twentieth century, especially 1950 onward, are the main feature here.
(right)
PASCAL CUISINIER, PAUL BERT MARKET, AISLE 6, STALL 91
A "Lentille" ceramic vase by Jacques and Danielle Ruelland (circa 1955) placed on a rosewood cabinet by Raphaël Raffel, 1956–57.

(above) GILLES OUDIN, PAUL BERT MARKET, AISLE 7, STALL 405

A longtime dealer at *les puces*, Gilles Oudin made industrial furniture popular—and vice versa! Pictured here, the earliest non-stackable Tolix chairs (1925–1937) in front of a table made from a workshop top and a pommel horse base. Behind it, a metallic blind by Dominique Perrault from the François Mitterand reading room of the National Library of France.

(opposite) MICHEL PERACHES AND ÉRIC MIELE, PAUL BERT MARKET, AISLE 1, STALL 21

Larger than life: An imposing bell, created for an opera set, is made of distressed polystyrene. On the same scale, but made of real oak, a display case from a store is more than fourteen feet wide and nearly ten feet high. In other words, items that are unlikely to go unnoticed.

(above) **SERPETTE MARKET, AISLE 1, STALL 41**
At the foot of a spiral staircase, an industrial style metal cabinet awaits a buyer.
(opposite) **LUDOVIC MESSAGER, QUINTESSENCE, 14, RUE PAUL BERT**
To be or not to be… This statue of a bather, made of polychrome terra-cotta, is believed to be the creation of Pablo Picasso.
She stands on a riveted metal console and is surrounded by lamps made from cast-iron blocks (circa 1890). Behind her, a clock face from the same period.

(preceding pages) **MICHEL PERACHES AND ÉRIC MIELE, PAUL BERT MARKET, AISLE 1, STALL 21**
A thousand lights shine from this star-shaped outdoor ornament, a Christmas decoration from the 1960s (made up of fifty 25-watt bulbs).
These eight-foot-tall letters made of Plexiglas and neon were used for a supermarket in the 1950s; the infrared lamps come from
an early-twentieth-century garage; and the stack of leather exercise mats dates from the 1920s.

LUDOVIC MESSAGER, QUINTESSENCE, 3, RUE PAUL BERT
A pair of riveted bookcases with a galvanized gray finish (circa 1900); a collection of brass and bronze Louis XIII–style candleholders. At both locations, Quintessence Lifestyle and Quintessence Playground, this dealer favors the excessive.

MICHEL PERACHES AND ÉRIC MIELE, PAUL BERT MARKET, AISLE 1, STALL 21
(opposite) A Levallois articulated lamp and a film projector from the 1920s set the stage for the contrast between a massive sculptor's stand and a rococo shell armchair of warm wood with gold and silver gilding (circa 1850–80).

(following pages)
(left) **JEAN-MICHEL CARPENTIER, PAUL BERT MARKET, AISLE 1, STALL 9**
For the past three years, this specialist in antique lamps has turned his attention to transforming recycled airplane parts into design objects and furniture. He uses propellers, wheels—even pieces of cabin fuselage. An inspired designer, he also appreciates older pieces, such as this Venetian mirror from the late nineteenth century.
(right) **MICHEL PERACHES AND ÉRIC MIELE, PAUL BERT MARKET, AISLE 1, STALL 21**
A mid–nineteenth century winepress base, made of iron, will soon be used for a completely different purpose.

(above) **GÉRARD MIZEL, SERPETTE MARKET, AISLE 1, STALL 41**
Mickey Mouse was spotted here, and many other stars can be seen each weekend, walking through the markets in their sunglasses.

(opposite) **DAVID MAHIEUX-ATTIA, PAUL BERT MARKET, AISLE 4, STALL 154**
Is this the former workshop of an electrician?

JEAN-MICHEL CARPENTIER, PAUL BERT MARKET, AISLE 1, STALL 9
Don't even try to figure this out: These hanging metal pieces are not the creations of a designer but parts of vintage airplanes reconfigured by the inventive Carpentier.

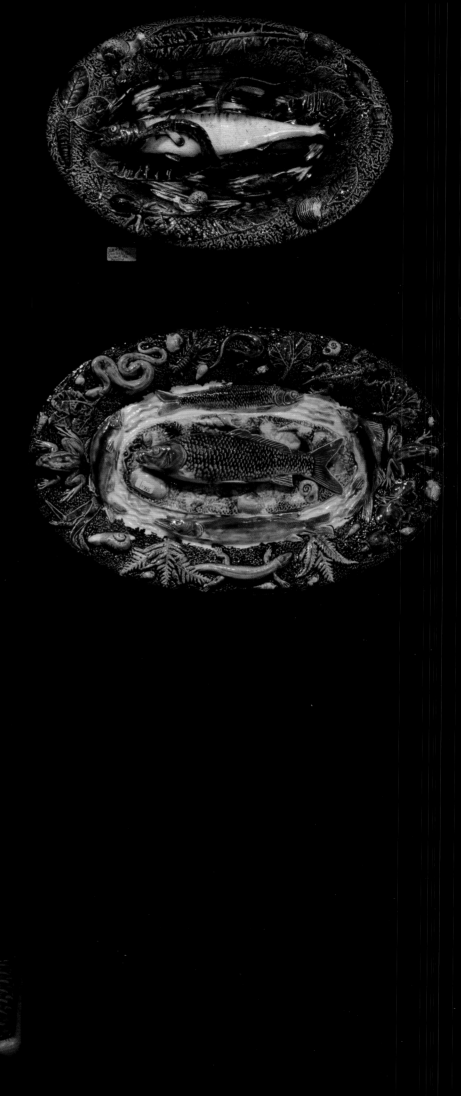

CHAPTER 4

LAURENCE VAUCLAIR, AIDJOLATE, PAUL BERT MARKET, AISLE 6, STALL 79
A nineteenth-century plaster *écorché* figure, set on a wicker stand
from a winter garden (circa late nineteenth or early twentieth century);
ceramic platters in the manner of Bernard Palissy.

THE
UNUSUAL

SYLVIE CORBELIN
Paul Bert Market, aisle 7, stall 291 bis

Dreamlike, strange, startling, amusing—we are entering the realm of curiosities. Women dealers are a strong presence in this area. Sylvie Corbelin, a jewelry and precious stones expert with a degree in gemology, designs many of the items in her shop at the Paul Bert Market. She says she learned her business "as she went along" and relies on instinct, favoring "materials that are rough and bizarre," such as lacquered wood, exotic cameos, coral, jade, meteorites, pearls, and turquoise, rather than "polished gold and cut diamonds." Her rings, bracelets, necklaces, and cuff links are ornate, colorful, and poetic, infused with mythology and wonder. Corbelin's collections have names such as Voyage to Babylon, Green Hell, or Highly Enlightened, giving them a tasteful audacity that suits the atmosphere of *les puces*.

ISABELLE MALEVAL
Dauphine Market, Sainte-Sophie aisle, stall 23

Authenticity and unexpected materials are also the leitmotif at Isabelle Maleval's shop, Présents Passés, in the Dauphine Market. She specializes in old tools, and there is mystery behind the disciplined perfection of the objects made of wood, leather, steel, or stone. What is that beautifully carved frieze? A yoke for a cow. Is that a sandstone monolith? No, it's a stonecutter's tooth chisel. A mirror mounted on a wood handle? It's actually a lark's lure, a marvelous bird decoy whose poetic name has been passed down to posterity. Every object has a purpose. "When I don't know the function of a piece, I keep it in front of me and wait for it to speak to me," says Maleval. Form united to function. Japanese shoemakers looking to buy old precision tools are among her devoted clients.

HERVÉ GOASGUEN, PAUL BERT MARKET AISLE 1, STALL 39 Printer's letters, metal pigeonholes, military mattresses, articulated chairs and lamps—for this dealer, vintage spirit is synonymous with utilitarian design.

PIERRE BAZALGUES, PAUL BERT MARKET, AISLE 4, STALL 211

(preceding pages) Taxidermy, anatomical engraving, a large metal medicine bottle from the nineteenth century—a selection of curiosities and vanitas typical of this dealer.

(above) Three plaster anatomical models from 1900 give this stall the aura of a medical school from the past.

(opposite) A stone skull, a macabre scene made of resin, a papier-mâché mummy, and many other curiosities with an archaeological bent.

MARTA BRYL

Serpette Market, aisle 1, stall 16

Curiosity knows no borders. Marta Bryl wrote a dissertation on the contemporary history of the Irish Republican Army, yet, she says, her revelation about archaeology came to her during a visit to the Greek Antiquities section of the British Museum in London. This is her area of concentration at the Serpette Market, with a preference for ceramics: Etruscan Bucchero Nero, the heavy, color-impregnated Greek artifacts in black glaze pottery "that inspired Cocteau and Picasso," as well as "ancient objects from before the time of Jesus Christ, and still modern today," she asserts.

LUCAS RATTON

Vernaison Market, aisle 1, stall 47

The same applies to African archaeology and primitive arts in general, as presented by Lucas Ratton, a very young (he is twenty-two) dealer in the Vernaison Market. His atavism is hereditary: His father, Philippe Ratton, a leading expert in the field, started out in the same market. Even the preceding generation (Maurice and Charles Ratton) had been in the business at the time of the cubists and surrealists, led by André Breton. Ratton describes his stall as "a nonsectarian meeting place," where he sells masks, statuettes, terra-cotta, and textiles. His stall fits perfectly into the eclecticism of *les puces*.

PATRICK AYME

Malassis Market, La Collectionnite, stall 5

Extreme curiosity often begins in childhood—witness Marcel Proust's madeleine. In that spirit, Patrick Ayme sells only antique toys in his Malassis Market location. His personal favorites are those dating from 1850 through the 1950s, toys made of painted or lithographed tin, as well as first-generation Japanese toy robots (1950–1970). In the mix are dolls by the illustrator Raymond Peynet. Ayme began collecting in "a former life, in the 1970s" to decorate the restaurant he owned at the time in Annemasse, in Haute-Savoie, and got caught up in the game, metamorphosing from collector to dealer.

YVAN DEVLAY

Paul Bert Market, aisle 5, stalls 235 and 237

FRANÇOIS DANECK COLONIAL CONCEPT 8, RUE PAUL BERT Coral, shells, and sea fans from the Solomon Islands, the Philippines, and the South Seas—this shop overflows with treasures from the ocean floor.

Ayme's is not an isolated case. Before opening his thriving curiosity shop in the Paul Bert Market, Yvan Devlay traveled extensively. Born in Egypt to a father who was also a collector, he began buying at a very young age and has a vivid memory of the auction of King Farouk's art collection, following

the military coup d'état in 1952 that overthrew the monarch. Later he studied in Paris and spent some time in Asia before settling at *les puces* in Saint-Ouen, "only for the past twenty-two years." All the objects in his "Oriental"-themed stall are "different in style and tone." Devlay likes to amuse the passersby with a life-size bulldog at the front of his shop.

PIERRE BAZALGUES
Paul Bert Market, aisle 4, stall 211

Another unusual story is that of Pierre Bazalgues. He was a nursery school teacher for twenty years before turning his attention, heart and soul, to vanitas, natural science objects, astronomical instruments, taxidermy, skulls, and skeletons, or, as he describes them, objects of "sweet folly." Among his clients are many European artists who come seeking a romantic, mysterious, or fantastic object that might spark their imagination, along with those who are simply collectors of appealing neo-Gothic objects or armillary spheres.

DAVID DOUSSY
Serpette Market, aisle 4, stall 2

Finally, stumbling upon a unique object can set one off down collecting's slippery slope. "There I was, a young *bobo* [bohemian-bourgeois] with a designer loft. One day, when I was at the flea market, I bought a scrap metal box. It was, in fact, a metal box from the fifteenth century." And that is how the amiable David Doussy started out in the business. He now deals in pre-Columbian art, objects from the Belle Époque, scientific instruments, and sixteenth-century talismans "with secret powers," such as crayfish eyes or a rhinoceros tooth. "Anything that can put you in a trance," says Doussy. Dreamers and those who love tales from long ago: Look no further. You have come to the right place.

LUDOVIC MESSAGER,
QUINTESSENCE,
3 & 14, RUE PAUL BERT
(preceding pages)
On these shelves, this antique dealer has assembled
a few interesting fragments recalling an old-fashioned
and somewhat alarming medicine cabinet!
(opposite)
In both his stalls, Messager specializes in oversize items.
Here, a table of riveted metal (circa 1900) is over 13 feet long.
The fishnet is also exceptionally large, as are the stools,
the shelves, and the banquette in the Gustavian style.
(following pages)
All manner of interesting objects are scattered on top
of an industrial workbench from the 1900s.

PIERRE BAZALGUES, PAUL BERT MARKET, AISLE 4, STALL 211

(opposite) An hourglass, a small casket, and a demonic candlestick from the nineteenth century: this dealer collects objects that illustrate the cruelty of, or perhaps the fascination with, the passing of time.

(following pages) Situated among all the shops dedicated to twentieth-century design, this one stands apart. The dark sciences, death, and vanitas fill every corner of this space, from the overflowing shelves of the pharmacy cabinet to the top of the neo-Gothic ladder. Artists from all over the world come here seeking inspiration or a shock to the senses.

MEUBLES ET OBJETS DE LA FORÊT NOIRE, PAUL BERT MARKET, AISLE 1, STALL 122
Wildlife art, bentwood furniture, decorative objects, deer horn lamps, and chandeliers represent the charming
and eclectic side of the Paul Bert Market. This is *the* ad hoc spot for those lucky enough to own a chalet in the mountains,
a cabin in the woods, or, better yet, a chic bungalow.

(following pages)
PIERRE BAZALGUES, PAUL BERT MARKET, AISLE 4, STALL 211
An ephemeral setting: A photograph from the 1900s showing the interior of a cathedral serves as a backdrop
for a leopard travel chair (circa 1940), a pair of candelabras, and a nineteenth-century neo-Gothic chair.
A twentieth-century mirrored console becomes an altar for a most unusual mass.

SARAH ROZENBAUM, LE PASSAGE MARKET, 18, RUE JULES-VALLÈS
Silk chiffon, lace, embroidered organdy, and tulle evoke the elegance of the period between 1925 and 1930.
In the world of fashion, this boutique is an institution, *the* go-to place for many designers. Lingerie, trimmings, dresses, ribbons, bags—treasures dating from the eighteenth to the twentieth centuries can be found in several of its stalls.

(preceding pages)
CHEZ CHANTAL, PAUL BERT MARKET, AISLE 1, STAND 71
Stylish shoes from the beginning of the last century; the surprised glance of a little blue-eyed face.

ALAIN BERTHON, TRÈS À L'ÉTROIT, SERPETTE MARKET, AISLE 3, STALL 13

Enameled, monogrammed, covered in animal skin or in the best art deco style—these lighters will help you light up in utmost elegance.
Also found here: fountain pens and other writing instruments, this dealer's specialty.

ALAIN AND HELEN ZISUL, LE MONDE DU VOYAGE, SERPETTE MARKET, AISLE 3, STALL 15

(above) This address appears in every chic guidebook, and fashionistas from around the world turn up here.

Two generations of the Zisul family have assembled the best of the best, the dream team designers of leather goods and travel accessories: Goyard, Hermès, and Louis Vuitton. More restrained shoppers will choose a handbag for every day; others will go all out with a steamer trunk for extended travel plans.

(opposite) The inimitable, timeless Kelly bag from Hermès; pictured here, a vintage model.

(above and opposite) **SYLVIE CORBELIN, PAUL BERT MARKET, AISLE 7, STALL 291**
With names like Prophetess, The Spirit of the Mamba, Nocturnal Sorceress, Eternal Life, Good Trip, Stromboli, La Palatine, Adamante, and Lady Lilith, all the inspired jewelry created by this dealer exudes a touch of mystery. Combining precious and semiprecious stones with metals and antique relics, these pieces are one of a kind or made in very limited quantities. Don't pass them up!

(preceding pages) **CLAUDE-ANNIE MARZET, SERPETTE MARKET**
A composition of ceramic fruits and vegetables (circa 1940–1950), assembled during this dealer's time at the Serpette, and a red lacquer and gold panel attributed to Pierre Bobot (circa 1940).

(above) **NICOLAS GIOVANNONI, SERPETTE MARKET, AISLE 6, STALLS 8 AND 10**
A recognized specialist in tabletop accessories for more than twenty years, this dealer has been a pillar of the Serpette Market. His merchandise—etched crystal glasses and decanters, porcelain and faience dishes, sets of silverware—is flawless. People come from as far away as Japan to admire his treasures from Baccarat, Bernardaud, Christofle, Ercuis, Haviland, Lalique, Puiforcat, and Saint-Louis, among others.

(opposite) **ANTIQUITÉS DE L'AUTHIE, PAUL BERT MARKET, AISLE 4, STALL 201**
This Paul Bert shop shares its name with a bucolic river in northern France. Here you can find engraved crystal pieces as well as more basic glassware, along with silver chalices to suit flea market habitués who like both the sacred and the profane.

ÉMAIL & PUCES, PAUL BERT MARKET, AISLE 2, STALL 36
Recapture the flavor of time gone by with promotional objects and toys from the past—a nostalgic escape for those who remain children at heart.

(preceding pages)
BACHELIER ANTIQUITÉS, PAUL BERT MARKET, AISLE 1, STALL 17
Choose the slender eight-ounce *fillette* or the more rounded sixteen-ounce *dames-jeannes* carafes. With a wide variety of antique glassware,
this stall is the place to go for culinary objects and furnishings: butcher's blocks, stoves, pottery, and wicker baskets, as well as wine-making tools.
François Bachelier is always eager to share anecdotes about his business.

DANIEL MERCIER, DU BILLARD AU COMPTOIR, SERPETTE MARKET, AISLE 4, STALL 8
A baraque board game (late nineteenth century) for French billiard fans, in particular, and those who appreciate beautiful objects, in general!

(preceding pages)
JEAN-MARC GAY, PAUL BERT MARKET, AISLE 2, STALL 141
Furnishings, sculptures, trophies, and other antique sports-related items are featured here. Many of these accessories are quite decorative, for those who want to lift weights—vintage style.

DANIEL MERCIER, DU BILLARD AU COMPTOIR, SERPETTE MARKET, AISLE 4, STALL 9

(above) The name of this shop says it all: An atmosphere of soft-lit nostalgia reigns here, as on a Michel Audiard film set.

(opposite) Game accessories, billiard sets (American and French versions), tender green opaline lamps, champagne buckets, bar stools—beautiful objects at reasonable prices.

FRANÇOIS-MICHEL HILDERAL, MOMENTS ET MATIÈRES, VERNAISON MARKET, AISLE 1, STALLS 13 AND 27
(above) Nineteenth-century parchment books, an antler chandelier, a polished steel ball, a large nineteenth-century table from Vietnam, botanical prints (circa 1828), a pair of wood tritons (circa 1940) used as lamp bases…
(opposite) This talented decorator and antiques dealer, François-Michel Hilderal, champions the mix of "extravagant genres."

FRANÇOIS DANECK, COLONIAL CONCEPT, 8, RUE PAUL BERT
An improvised scene in front of a door that once belonged to a sixteenth-century French brothel: the juxtaposition of four Ethiopian Kongo funerary pots and several mounted animals (a lion, a vulture, a zebu) taking down a waterbuck.

FRANÇOIS DANECK, COLONIAL CONCEPT, 8, RUE PAUL BERT

(above) A Fang mask from Gabon, a ceremonial Iroquois headdress, and a fossilized pterodactyl wing (seventy million years old) sit among other items on a colonial roll-top desk from Cuba; on the wall, a portrait of a Mangbetu man painted by Gaston Lesuisse, circa 1930s.

(opposite) Fashion meets decor: A Sioux headdress and tunic from the late nineteenth century; an early-twentieth-century Inuit parka made of marine mammal intestines; a Napoleon III–era sofa covered in weathered leather; nesting tables of Makassar ebony and wenge with mahogany legs.

FRANÇOIS DANECK, COLONIAL CONCEPT, 8, RUE PAUL BERT

(above) The exotic den of a taxidermist, with several mounted animals: an African buffalo, a giraffe, and a cheetah.

(opposite) An unusual mix: cotton and Kuba fabric curtains from the Democratic Republic of Congo; a coverlet made of orylag fur; nesting tables in lacquer and zebra skin; a sofa and chairs covered in astrakhan, designed by François Daneck.

FRANÇOIS DANECK, COLONIAL CONCEPT, 8, RUE PAUL BERT

(opposite) This could be the mysterious palace of an explorer. On the wall, an imposing late-nineteenth-century panel made of six hundred azulejos shows Christopher Columbus standing before the Catholic kings after his return from the Americas. Other furnishings and objects include a leather Chesterfield sofa from the early twentieth century; a stool made of bronze and zebra skin, designed by François Daneck; and a ceramic vase by Antonio da Silva.

(following pages) Walls weathered by sand and embellished with coconut fibers; a Napoleon III–era sofa covered with a fabric by Aissa Dione; a Bambara mask; a sculpture from Sepik, in Papua New Guinea; table lamps made of crocodile skin; and a bedcover embroidered with butterflies, designed by François Daneck. Protected by a mosquito net and removed from the danger of wild animals, this beautiful bedroom rivals those of the grandest African lodges.

OVERVIEW
OF THE MARKETS

The covered stalls, open-air bazaars, streets, and alleys of the Saint-Ouen flea markets truly form a city within a city. They're a world of archaeological artifacts; silver; African, American, and Asian art; bric-a-brac; vintage jewelry; wood paneling; books; furniture; photographs; paintings; glassworks; and more. Here are a few guidelines, then, to help you navigate the maze of styles and objects in the sixteen separate markets. These are the best of the lot. Keep in mind that *les puces* are a living marketplace, so vendors often move, and business hours can fluctuate.

THE GRANDDADDY: THE VERNAISON MARKET
(99, RUE DES ROSIERS, AND 136, AVENUE MICHELET)

This is where it all started at the beginning of the last century. The Vernaison Market has a chic and bohemian spirit. Its winding aisles offer myriad interesting items for all kinds of collectors, such as dishes featuring the head of Napoleon I, for those nostalgic for the First Empire (Philippe Pellerin, aisle 1, stalls 18–20); Bakelite flowers to help lovers declare their eternal devotion (Tombées du Camion, aisle 5, stall 92); and promotional key chains from the 1960s for avid collectors of mid-century memorabilia (Françoise Chappuy, aisle 5, stall 88). Only an ascetic could resist such temptation!

NOT TO BE MISSED: THE SERPETTE MARKET
(110, RUE DES ROSIERS)

The name itself is a label. This is the place to be for trendy merchandise. An international clientele, American interior designers in particular, flocks to this market of specialized and general dealers, looking for travel accessories bearing the monograms of famous luggage manufacturers (Monde du Voyage, aisle 3, stall 15) or a piece of jewelry that was designed for a movie star in the heyday of Hollywood (Olwen Forest, aisle 3, stalls 5 and 7).

THE LATEST FADS IN INTERIORS: THE PAUL BERT MARKET
(18, RUE PAUL BERT, AND 96, RUE DES ROSIERS)

The resurgence of many of the twentieth century's decorative arts styles began here, including art deco, 1940s style, 1950s design, and vintage Scandinavian. Several Parisian antiques experts also started out at the Paul Bert Market: Alexandre Biaggi, Philippe Jousse, Jacques Lacoste, Pierre Passebon, and, of course, the aforementioned Marc-Antoine Pâtissier. This market is always at the forefront of new trends in the decorative arts. Some dealers are "specialists within a specialty," such as Nicolas Denis (aisle 2, stall 40), who is particularly keen on furniture from the second half of the twentieth century by designers such as Martin Boileau, Louis Durot, Richard Guino, Philolaos Tloupas, Takis Vassilakis, and Claude Viseux.

THE PICTURESQUE: THE JULES-VALLÈS MARKET
(7, RUE JULES-VALLÈS)

Established in 1938, this is the oldest covered market at *les puces*. Somewhat removed from the center of activity, the Jules-Vallès Market has always reflected the true spirit of a flea market. Within its two small aisles, you can find everything and anything, in a mix of styles and genres offered by traditional dealers such as Patrick and Gérard Parent (aisle 1, stalls 37, 39, 55, 57, and 59) and the well-known gallerist Éric Philippe, a respected specialist in French, American, Austrian, and Scandinavian decorative arts from the first half of the twentieth century.

THE ARISTOCRAT:
THE BIRON MARKET (85, RUE DES ROSIERS)

There are only two aisles in this important market and no sign of bric-a-brac. The stalls here are virtual galleries, proudly lined up. For a long time, the specialties of the Biron Market were gilt wood, signed furniture, and art objects from the eighteenth and nineteenth centuries. Today, the choices are more eclectic, with additions from the last century such as Régis Royant, who has two locations: One shop is devoted to the period between 1930 and 1950; the other features merchandise from the 1970s (aisle 1, stalls 24 and 33).

LITERARY:
THE DAUPHINE MARKET (140, RUE DES ROSIERS)

Established in 1991, the youngest of the markets is also one of the largest. It's famous for Bookshop Square, located on the second floor, with its old books, works of literature, works on paper, photographs, and vinyl record albums. Don't miss the Librairie Jacques Desse (stalls 208–213), a treasure trove of antique tab and pop-up books created for children of past centuries and collected by grown-up children today.

SUPERSIZE:
L'ENTREPÔT MARKET (80, RUE DES ROSIERS)

Knickknack lovers, stay away! This market sells only oversize, heavy, voluminous pieces, such as staircases, castle gates, garden pavilions, and entire sections of libraries—the stuff of stately homes and dreams.

UNDER THE RADAR: LE PASSAGE MARKET
(27, RUE LECUYER, AND 18, RUE JULES-VALLÈS)

Only insiders know about Chez Sarah, a clothing collector's paradise. This small shop belongs to Sarah Rozenbaum. The fashion world converges here, as designers and collectors come for inspiration or to uncover a rare jewel of a find, such as an embroidered purse, a remnant of satin brocade, some Valenciennes lace, a beaded trim, or chiffon dresses from the 1930s. From floor to ceiling, it's a nonstop fashion show.

THE STEAMSHIP:
THE MALASSIS MARKET (142, RUE DES ROSIERS)

With a double staircase and stalls lined up like cabins, the layout of this market is reminiscent of an ocean liner. One particular shop stands out among the rest: Erotic Secret (allée des Ebénistes, stalls 89–90), a place entirely devoted to erotic antiques from the Orient and other remote areas. You might find an African fertility amulet, a door knocker from a brothel, nineteenth-century dildos made of ivory, and a seventeenth-century phallus in Venetian glass, among other special objects.

VISITOR INFORMATION
The hours of operation posted by the Marchés aux Puces de Saint-Ouen are: Saturday, 9:00 a.m. to 6:00 p.m.; Sunday, 10:00 a.m. to 6:00 p.m.; and Monday, 11:00 a.m. to 5:00 p.m., but the schedule has been known to change.

USEFUL
ADDRESSES

BARS AND RESTAURANTS
• Le Paul Bert
20, rue Paul Bert
This café-restaurant with a terrace is ideally situate within reach of the antiques, at the very beginning of Aisle 1 of the Paul Bert Market. Typical bistro fare (stews are often served in small black Le Creuset pots) and brunch selections cater to early-risers as well as those who sleep in.

• La Chope des Puces
122, rue des Rosiers
The rue des Rosiers, the central axis for most of the flea markets, is also the home of La Chope des Puces, a famous jazz café. Fans of Django Reinhardt gather here—especially on weekends, when the neighborhood is in full swing—to listen to guitarists and other musicians. Check the schedule posted on the window.

HARDWARE STORE
Produits Dugay
92, rue des Rosiers
Tel: 01 40 11 87 30
www.produits-dugay.com
Opened in 1950, this *puces* institution sells a thousand and one products for maintaining and restoring furniture and artifacts. Could there be a better location for such an establishment? Wood, leather, gilding, marble, metal—these experts can handle it all. In fact, they invented Pâte Dugay, the miraculous furniture wax.

SHIPPING COMPANIES (for both domestic and international shipping)
• Camard, Paul Bert Market, tel: 01 40 12 84 45
• Détroit, tel: 01 40 12 91 53; www.detroit-demenageurs.fr
• Edet International, Biron Market, tel: 01 49 45 07 17; www.edetinternational.com

FRANÇOIS DANECK, COLONIAL CONCEPT, 8, RUE PAUL BERT
"I am a big kid," says François Daneck, which might explain the presence of the horse on wheels from Cuba in the 1950s.
Behind it, an early-twentieth-century screen covered with chromo advertising cards for chocolate products.

BIBLIOGRAPHY

Baudot, François. *Chanel.* Paris: Assouline, 1998.

Bethenod, Martin. *Jacques Kerchache, portraits croisés, entretiens, texte et images réunis.* Paris: Gallimard/Musée du Quai Branly, 2003.

Breton, André. *Mad Love.* Translated by Mary Ann Caws. Lincoln and London: University of Nebraska Press, 1987.

Breton, André. *Nadja.* Translated by Richard Howard. New York: Grove Press, 1960.

Breton, André, 42, rue Fontaine. Auction catalogue for sale organized by the Hôtel Drouot and Calmels Cohen. Paris: H.-C. Randier, 2003.

Buot, François. *Nancy Cunard.* Paris: Fayard/Pauvert, 2008.

Calmus, Jean. *Guide des puces de Saint-Ouen et de Paris.* Paris: Albin Michel, 1977.

Capia, Robert. *Les Petits Objets de collection.* Paris: Stock, 1971.

Chalon, Jean. *Florence et Louise les magnifiques: Florence Jay-Gould et Louise de Vilmorin.* Paris: Éditions du Rocher, 1987.

Charles-Roux, Edmonde. *Le Temps Chanel.* Paris: Chêne/Grasset, 1985.

Delay, Claude. *Chanel solitaire.* Paris: Gallimard, 1983.

Dollfus, Ariane. *Noureev: l'insoumis.* Paris: Flammarion, 2007.

Dufresne, Jean-Luc. *Christian Dior… homme du siècle.* Versailles: Artlys, 2005.

Gaillemin, Jean-Louis. *Antiquaires.* Paris: Assouline, 2000.

Galante, Pierre. *Les Années Chanel. Paris Match*/Paris: Mercure de France, 1972.

Kochno, Boris. *Christian Bérard.* Paris: Herscher, 1987.

La Maison Paul. Connaissance des Arts, special edition no. 295. Paris: Société Française de Promotion Artistique, 2009.

Liaut, Jean-Noël. *Madeleine Castaing: mécène à Montparnasse, décoratrice à Saint-Germain-des Prés.* Paris: Payot, 2008.

Mauriès, Patrick. *Louise de Vilmorin: un album.* Paris: Le Promeneur, 2002.

Meyer-Stabley, Bertrand. *Noureev.* Paris: Éditions Payot et Rivages, 2003.

Pochna, Marie-France. *Christian Dior.* Paris: Flammarion, 1993.

Prévert, Jacques. *Paroles: Selected Poems.* Translated by Lawrence Ferlinghetti. San Francisco: City Lights Books, 1990.

Rabourdin, Elie, and Alice Chavane. *Je suis couturier, propos receuillis.* Paris: Éditions du Conquistador, 1951.

Ternon, François. *Histoire du No. 5 de Chanel: un numéro intemporel.* Nantes: Normant, 2009.

Tessarech, Bruno. *Villa Blanche.* Paris: Gallimard/Folio, 2007.

Vilmorin, Louise de, Duff Cooper, and Diana Cooper. *Correspondance à trois (1944–1953).* Paris: Le Promeneur, 2008.

Wagener, Françoise. *Je suis née inconsolable: Louise de Vilmorin (1902–1969).* Paris: Albin Michel, 2008.

VERNAISON MARKET, AISLE 6, STALL 110BIS
As the granddaddy of all the markets in Saint-Ouen, the Vernaison has retained the authentic spirit of antiquing. An assortment of merchandise is presented in all simplicity, as seen here: picture frames hung randomly on a gate, offered even before the curtain goes up!

PHOTO CREDITS

All photographs by Laziz Hamani, except as noted below:
  - page 10: Luc Fournol/Photo 12
  - page 17: Collection Centre Pompidou, Dist. RMN/Philippe Migeat. © Estate Gisèle Freund/
        IMEC Images
  - pages 18-19: Collection Centre Pompidou, Dist. RMN/Philippe Migeat
  - page 20: Georgette Chadourne/PFB/Rue des Archives ; © ADAGP, Paris 2010
  - page 22: Richard Kalvar/Magnum Photos
  - page 23: Jaussaud-Seuillet/Gamma
  - page 24: Sophie Bassouls/Sygma/Corbis
  - page 25: Boris Lipnitzki/Roger-Viollet
  - page 26: Horst P. Horst/Art + Commerce
  - page 27: Henri-Cartier Bresson/Magnum Photos

ACKNOWLEDGMENTS

The author would like to thank Alexandre Biaggi, Armand Les Saulniers, Edith Lory, Nicholas Moufflet, Marie Palatine, Marc-Antoine Pâtissier, Philippe Pellerin, Eric Philippe, and Yvette Tourneloup.

The photographer wishes to thank Martine and Prosper Assouline for the opportunity to do what he loves and for entrusting him with this book; it was a true adventure and brought him pure joy. Thank you to Yohann Gendry, without whom he could not have taken these many images. His presence was invaluable.
Thank you to all the dealers for their good-humored cooperation and for the time spent so that he might discover their magical world.
Thank you to Edith Lory for her participation and immeasurable help.
Thank you to Nathan Ronny for his assistance and to Laure Verchère for her keen eye and magnificent writing.
Thank you to Romuald Habert and Digitaline for their role in the finalization of the images.
And finally, many thanks to the entire Assouline team for their work and participation.

The editor wishes to thank Laure Verchère, as well as Laziz Hamani and his assistant, Yohann Gendry. He also thanks, for their image research, Eva Bodinet (Magnum Photos), Françoise Carminati (Corbis), Magali Galtier (Eyedea), Véronique Garrigues and Anita Pognon (ADAGP), Bruno Pouchin (Roger-Viollet), Laurence Kersuzan and Pierrick Jan (RMN), Melissa Regan (Art + Commerce), Mélina Reynaud (IMEC Images), Catherine Terk (Rue des Archives), and Claudine Zuzinec (Photo 12).

Metro Garibaldi

rue Louis Darn
l'Entrepôt
rue des Rosiers
l'Usine
Paul Bert
rue des Bons Enfants
Jules Vallès
rue Kléber
rue de la Gaîté
l'écurie
rue du Plaisir
rue neuve Pierre Curie
rue Jules Vallès
le Passage
rue Charles Schmidt
rue l'écurie